1 As a result of visiting the Ruskin Museum at Walkley Benjamin Creswick became a professional sculptor. This is his 1877 bust of John Ruskin which was presented to Prince Leopold.

1 *Ruskin's vision*

> I have listened to many ingenious persons, who say we are better off now than ever we were before. I do not know how well off we were before; but I know positively that many very deserving persons of my acquaintance have great difficulty in living under these improved circumstances; also, that my desk is full of begging letters, eloquently written either by distressed or dishonest people; and that we cannot be called, as a nation, well off, while so many of us are living either in honest or in villainous beggary.
>
> For my own part, I will put up with this state of things, passively, not an hour longer.

Thus wrote John Ruskin in January 1871 in the first of his "Letters to the Workmen and Labourers of Great Britain" which he called *Fors Clavigera*. He announced that he was going to set aside some small part of his income to assist "in what one and all we shall have to do". He urged everyone to help in establishing "a National Store instead of a National Debt".

By 1871 John Ruskin was a national figure. His book *Modern Painters* had established him as a great writer on art and an art critic. The chapter in his *Stones of Venice* on "The Nature of Gothic", where he looked at the lot of the craftsman, was hailed by William Morris as "one of the few necessary and inevitable utterances of the century". In 1860 his book *Unto this Last* launched him securely into the field of social and political economy. He was a great lecturer, and by now Slade Professor of Fine Art in the university of Oxford. Ruskin is accepted as one of the greatest Victorians.

Through succeeding pages of *Fors Clavigera* Ruskin continued to develop his ideas. In order to better the lot of the greater mass of the people, Ruskin hoped that his readers would generously give money or land to his new St George's Company. His original concept was to show how much food could be grown on barren or neglected land. The Company was to acquire such land and employ labourers to work it. Other land, not owned by the Company, would be managed and cultivated in the same way by "Companions".

He hoped that on the Company's land, or on that of Companions, communities would grow up, each with its own school where children would be taught the laws of justice, patriotism and domestic happiness, with such subjects as music, geometry, astronomy, botany, zoology, history, drawing, carpentry and pottery. The community and school would have its own library and art gallery.

Ruskin was tenacious, and adapted his various ideas to suit new circumstances. In his pamphlet on *The Employment of the Destitute and Criminal Classes* in 1868 he had included the "Bringing in of waste land" as one of the classes of work which bodies of men could be organised into doing.

The St George's Fund was established – its prime purpose was to buy land – and Ruskin's friends, Sir Thomas Acland and William Cowper-Temple were appointed its trustees. Ruskin began the Fund with his own donation of £7000. But other gifts of land or money were disappointingly slow to materialise. The first gift of land was made in 1875 by one of the Guild's first

Companions, Mrs Fanny Talbot. She gave a group of eight cottages on a steep hillside at Barmouth in North Wales. Mrs Talbot was later to become one of the National Trust's first benefactors, giving that organisation more land at Barmouth.

The "Company" (the group of supporters who banded together to support Ruskin's ideals) and the "Fund" (the account holding the donations received) eventually merged and

4 Photographed on the frozen Lake Coniston in January 1879, Ruskin with Mrs Talbot.

developed into St George's Guild and in 1875 the lawyers examined the legal implications of establishing a company. Eventually a solution was found in the Companies Act of 1867, and in July 1875 the first draft of the Constitution was prepared. Legal wrangling continued for some time and in August

1878 the "Application for a licence of the Board of Trade" was published. In October the Memorandum and Articles of Association were filed and a week later the licence was granted. We had become one of the earliest limited liability companies and grudgingly the Board of Trade allowed us not to be called The Guild of St George *Limited.*

While the legal niceties were being worked on, the Guild was making progress. In Birmingham, George Baker had a distinguished record of achievement in public life. In 1870 the Crown sold land in Worcestershire – Winterdyne and Tickenhill in the manor of Bewdley – and Baker bought

5 *George Baker, Master, 1900-1910*

some 381 acres. He was planning to build his house, Beaucastle, here and his architect incorporated many of Ruskin's ideas into its design. Baker clearly thought highly of Ruskin and early in 1871 he had offered Ruskin seven acres of his woodland at Bewdley. The offer was later increased to twenty acres and the gift was formally accepted once the Guild was legally established. In 1877 Baker became mayor of Birmingham. He invited Ruskin to visit him at his home at Bellefield there and on the following day he took Ruskin to Bewdley to see the twenty acres of land, and Beaucastle which was probably still being built.

Meanwhile, a former member of Ruskin's art class at London's Working Men's College, Henry Swan, had settled in Sheffield and had been corresponding with Ruskin about the Guild. In September 1875 Ruskin accepted his invitation to visit his home to meet a group of his Sheffield friends. By now Swan lived in Bellhag Road,

6 *The Guild's original museum at Walkley. The later extension can be seen at the rear.*

9

Walkley, on high ground to the north west of the city centre. They must have talked of Ruskin's plans for the Guild and that one of the plans included a museum. Ruskin was clearly impressed by his visit and on the same day he instructed his solicitors to buy the cottage. Ever prepared to adapt his plans to changing circumstances, Ruskin intended setting up the Guild's first museum in one room here, with Swan as its curator and with the Swan family occupying the rest of the cottage.

Ruskin wanted the hard-working men of the Sheffield steel industry to benefit from his museum and its contents and he liked the idea of the men walking up the hill from the smokey city centre into the cleaner air of Walkley, overlooking the countryside of the Rivelin valley; as he wrote, "not to keep the collection out of smoke, but expressly to beguile the artisan out of it".

In 1875 Weston House in Sheffield, which had been given to the town by the Misses Harrison was being converted into the city's first museum. The chairman of the Museums Committee was Alderman William Bragge. Bragge himself was a collector of, among many other things, medieval manuscripts. He sold his collection in 1876. Ruskin possibly did not know of its provenance when he bought from Bernard Quaritch the 12th century *Commentary on the Psalms*, and a 13th century Parisien *Bible*, formerly in Bragge's collection.

In August 1875 Ruskin announced in *Fors Clavigera* his intention "to place some books and minerals, as the germ of a museum arranged first for workers in iron, and extended into illustration of the natural history of the neighbourhood [of Sheffield], and more especially of the geology and flora of Derbyshire". Bragge became aware of Ruskin's intention, and wrote to him telling him of the already planned museum in Weston House. He offered Ruskin whatever space he might require in the building to house the Guild's collection.

Ruskin knew exactly what he wanted in his museum, and being aware of current museological thinking, he knew what to expect in Weston House. He replied to Bragge:

> My dear Sir, I am obliged by your note, but the work of the St George's Company is necessarily distinct from all other. My "museum" may be perhaps nothing but a two-windowed garret. But it will have nothing in it but what deserves respect in art or

admiration in nature. A great museum in the present state of the public mind is simply an exhibition of the possible modes of doing wrong in art, and an accumulation of uselessly multiplied ugliness in misunderstood nature. Our own museum at Oxford [the Oxford University Museum] is full of distorted skulls, and your Sheffield ironwork department will necessarily contain the most barbarous abortions that human rudeness can ever produce with human fingers. The capitals of the iron shafts in any railway station, for instance, are things to make a man wish – for shame of his species – that he had been born a dog or a bee. Ever faithfully yours, J.Ruskin

P.S. I have no doubt your geological department will be well done, and my poor little cabinets will enable your men to use it to better advantage, but would be entirely lost if united with it.

Bragge later quoted the private letter in his speech at the dinner held to celebrate the opening of Weston Park Museum, leading to a certain amount of ill-feeling!

7 St George's Farm, Totley, near Sheffield; Ruskin preferred to call it Abbeydale. It was bought in 1876.

Ruskin was in Sheffield again in April 1876. He had just had a new carriage built, and was posting from London to his home at Brantwood, Coniston, taking his cousin Joan and her husband Arthur Severn with him. He only seems to have been in Sheffield over night but he visited his new museum at

11

Walkley and according to Severn, he was disappointed at how cramped the "museum" space in the house was in relation to the material available for exhibition. Again, Swan had friends for Ruskin to meet. As a result of this meeting and the suggestion of Swan and his friends, Ruskin bought a thirteen acre farm at Totley on the outskirts of the city, where the men could work the land. Although they *wished* to work on the land, none had agricultural experience. There was a certain amount of internecine dispute before Ruskin engaged William Harrison Riley to take charge of affairs. Riley was a friend of Edward Carpenter, the writer on social subjects, but Ruskin's hope that he would be able to bring some measure of control to the workings of this St George's Farm were unfounded. Ruskin believed that Riley "liked smoking better than digging" and sent his old Head Gardener, David Downs, to Totley to take charge, and Riley emigrated to America. Some of the men who had originally wanted to farm also left, but Downs ran the farm with some small degree of success for a number of years until Ruskin allowed the miner and quarry worker, George Pearson, to take it over. Pearson continued to run St George's Farm as a market garden and nursery for over fifty years, eventually buying the farm from the Guild in 1929. He died in 1938 aged eighty years and the farm was sold again. It is still called St George's Farm.

Meanwhile, the Guild's two trustees, Sir Thomas Acland and William Cowper-Temple, both thought that Ruskin was being very rash in buying the Totley land, and they both resigned. George Baker now became a trustee.

At about this time, Egbert Rydings had written to Ruskin drawing his attention to some errors in the Guild's accounts published in *Fors Clavigera*, and he was promptly appointed the Guild's accountant and Company Secretary. Rydings lived in the Isle of Man where he was developing a woollen business. Ruskin took a great interest in this and by 1879 Rydings had found an old water-powered corn mill at Laxey in which he had bought a part share, to make it into a small woollen mill. The Guild undertook to pay the annual rent and to pay £500

8 *St George's Woollen Mill at Laxey, from a sketch by Egbert Rydings.*

to equip the mill with its necessary looms, a small spinning mule, and other equipment. Rydings was convinced that in carding and weaving for the farms for ten miles around, the mill would be a success. And indeed it was a modest success, surviving for many years. Ruskin set the example by having some of his own clothes made from Laxey cloth, but as W. G. Collingwood pointed out, one of its chief drawbacks was that it never wore out! The mill is still working today, but now has no connection with the Guild.

The 1870s were busy times for investment in land. Companion John Guy wrote to Ruskin on Whit Sunday 1877 telling him that he had left his employment at Newby Hall Farm in Yorkshire because of over-mechanisation. Ruskin deplored the use of steam power. The outcome of the correspondence was that the Guild bought a small holding of thirteen acres and a cottage at Cloughton near Scarborough where Guy settled and farmed moderately successfully. In 1882 he gave up the tenancy after one of his sons drowned in a pond. He moved to Bewdley, settling at Long Bank, adjoining the Guild land, where he worked as a carpenter. In 1886 he emigrated to New Zealand. The farm at Cloughton was re-let and later sold.

Meanwhile Ruskin was furiously collecting and commissioning works of art for the Collection. In 1876 he paid £29 10s. for "Prints for Walkley"; in the following year he was commissioning pictures from Henry Stacy Marks and J.W.Bunney in Venice. In 1877 he paid £265 for unspecified "drawings" and he paid Arthur Burgess £84 for work at Rouen. In June 1877 Charles Fairfax Murray, with the help of J.W. Bunney, arranged for Ruskin to buy what was probably the Guild's most important acquisition. In the Manfrini Gallery in Florence Murray found a *Madonna and Child* by Andrea del Verrocchio, the Master of Leonardo, which was bought for £100. The Collection was growing rapidly.

9 The Guild commissioned Philippa Abrahams to make this replica of Verrocchio's Madonna and Child. She only used pigments available when the original was painted in the 15th century. Due to the deterioration of pigments in the original painting this looks more like the painting when it left Verrocchio's studio.

It was also in 1877 that Ruskin printed his first catalogue of the Collection; in the same year he published his *Abstract of the Objects and Constitution of St George's Guild* in which he explained that the Guild consisted of a body of people who thought that the sum that they usually set aside for charitable purposes might be most usefully "applied in buying land for the nation and entrusting the cultivation of it to a body of well-taught and well cared-for peasantry". For the teaching of these people "schools are to be erected, with museums and libraries in fitting places".

As Slade Professor at Oxford Ruskin had met and become friendly with the undergraduate Prince Leopold, the youngest son of Queen Victoria. In 1877 the prince visited the Guild's museum at Walkley and Ruskin spent thirty five minutes conducting his visitors around the Collection. He was introduced to the curator, Henry Swan, who had fostered the career of the young Sheffield sculptor, Benjamin Creswick. In conjunction with the royal visit, Prince Leopold was presented with Creswick's bust of Ruskin. George Baker was still completing his new house at Bewdley and he commissioned Creswick to carve some of the red sandstone of the external staircase, and to make some wrought iron decoration to go beneath a Gothic arch.

Unfortunately not all of those who believed in Ruskin's ideals and tried to follow them were entirely successful. James Burden was an intelligent Scottish engineer working in London. He became a Companion and his name is on the original 1876 Roll of Companions. He gave up his work as an engineer and tried to learn to work as an agricultural labourer. From earning thirty eight shillings a week, his wage dropped to twelve shillings. He had a mother and sister to support. Ruskin had denounced usury and Burden thought this enabled him to take liberties with the credit system. He forged two cheques by using Ruskin's name and at the end of March 1879 Ruskin had to give evidence against him in court. Burden was sentenced to a year in jail. At the end of this period Ruskin gave him the means to begin a better career and he seems to have become a printer.

Writing in 1882 in his *General Statement explaining the Nature and Purposes of St George's Guild*, Ruskin admitted that his original hopes for gifts of land for his agricultural experiments had not developed as he had hoped. The unavailability of land meant that the communities which Ruskin had envisaged developing on it did not happen. The schools which would have served these communities would have had their own museums. Always ready to adapt his plans Ruskin began giving books and works of art to existing educational establishments, in a way, developing the association which he had had with the girls' school run by Miss Bell at

10 The May Queen and her attendants and others at Whitelands College, Chelsea, in the 1890s.

Winnington Hall in Cheshire in the 'sixties. At Oxford he had endowed a Drawing Mastership and generously gave a teaching collection to the Drawing School. In the late 1870s he became interested in Whitelands College, then in Chelsea, and over the years gave them many books and pictures. Some Guild pictures were also loaned to Whitelands. From 1882 onwards he gave many books, including a 10th century Greek *Gospels* (now called *The Cheltenham Gospels*) to Cheltenham Ladies' College. At Oxford, Lady Margaret Hall and Somerville College also received gifts of books.

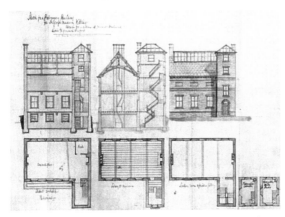

11 Plans by A.Hayball for a proposed extension to the Walkley Museum, 1882.

The emphasis of the Guild's work was turning from the development of land towards the further expansion of the Collection. In his *General Statement* Ruskin explained that the one room available in the Walkley house was quite inadequate for the display of the Collection. The architect A.Hayball drew plans for an extension to

15

the house, "two-storeyed and divided in each storey into a 'gallery' with a terminal attached 'room'. The lower (ground) storey, consisting of the Public Library with an attached students' reading-room, and the upper, or second floor, sky-lighted, consisting of the Art Gallery with attached Jewel Room".

When the good people of Sheffield heard of Ruskin's plans, they decided that even with the proposed extension the museum space would be inadequate and they proposed to build an entirely new museum to house the Collection. Attending his only Guild annual general meeting, at Oxford in 1884, Ruskin explained plans for future museum developments. Due to Ruskin's ill-health, negotiations temporarily faltered. Eventually, however, E. R. Robson drew plans for a new museum and the city promised £5000 towards the cost of the building. Ultimately the scheme foundered because it was not found to be possible to guarantee the Guild's ownership of the Collection, and in 1884 a single storey extension was added to the back of the Walkley building.

12 The interior of the extension to the Walkley Museum, with Bunney's painting of St Mark's, Venice, on the end wall.

In his *Master's Report* for 1885 Ruskin explained that due to lack of space at Walkley, some two thousand pounds-worth of drawings commissioned for the Guild were in store at his home at Brantwood or lent to various schools. He announced that he proposed to leave the museum at Walkley "as it stands" and build a new museum on Guild land "in the pure air of Bewdley". Plans for the proposed Bewdley building were drawn by Joseph Southall, the nephew of George Baker, and at about the same time E.R.Robson also drew plans for a Bewdley museum. Although the Bewdley museum was never built, the Guild was able to add Southall's plans to the Collection in 2007.

The London solicitor, Albert Fleming had given up city life in 1883 and had moved, with his housekeeper, Marian Twelves, to Neaum Crag near Ambleside. Fleming was a Companion and soon became one of Ruskin's inner circle of Lake District friends. About 1884, with Miss Twelves, Fleming set about reviving the rural spinning industry in Langdale. The daleswomen spun the locally-grown flax in their homes and the thread was hand-woven to make a very durable cloth. Ruskin took a great interest in this experiment, which was later taken under the Guild's wing and became known as the Ruskin Linen Industry.

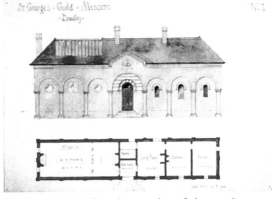

13 Joseph Southall made a number of plans and drawings for the Guild's proposed museum at Bewdley. This is one such drawing.

At about this same time a group of young people in Liverpool "discovered" Ruskin and established a Ruskin Society. Soon afterwards they became aware of the Guild, for two of the members of the new society, J. E. Fowler and Margaret Cox, were already Companions. Soon a group of them banded together to lease Mulberry Cottage, a cottage with a walled garden at Wavertree, and there the circle led a "Ruskinian" life, cultivating the garden, learning to spin, and engaging in "philosophical talk" over tea, toast and rhubarb. One of the key figures in the venture was Edith Hope Scott whose book *Ruskin's Guild of St George* (1931) chronicles much of the Guild's early history. Another was William Wardle, secretary to the Liverpool Ruskin Society, and later to play an important role in the life of the Guild.

14 William Wardle at Mulberry Cottage, Liverpool. He was Secretary of the Liverpool Ruskin Society and Secretary to the Guild, 1908-1925.

In 1883 the Birmingham architect and Guild trustee, J.H.Chamberlain, died. Quartus ("Quarry") Talbot, son of the Guild's early benefactor, was appointed trustee in his stead. Meanwhile the collection of pictures was growing apace, and in 1886 some of them were exhibited at The Fine Art Society in Bond Street. In the *Catalogue of a Series of Drawings made for St George's Guild under the Direction of Mr Ruskin*, Ruskin explained that the forty four drawings exhibited were characteristic "of between two and three hundred" so far bought for the Guild. The drawings included works by Angelo Alessandri, Frank Randal, Charles Fairfax Murray, T. M. Rook and W. G. Collingwood. The exhibition also included Robson's plans for the proposed Bewdley museum.

The years 1887-88 saw Ruskin suffering again from ill-health. He spent a number of months living at the seaside in Kent, and later in 1888 he undertook his final continental tour. He was unable to deal with business matters and the affairs of the Guild languished. Following a short visit to Seascale in Cumberland in 1889 Ruskin suffered a further illness which left him incapable of further work. Also in 1889 Quarry Talbot died and was replaced as trustee by George Thomson. Henry Swan, the Guild's curator and the original reason for the Collection being in Sheffield, also died.

Meanwhile in Sheffield the corporation had bought Meersbrook Park in 1886. The Collection needed new accommodation and with Ruskin unable to act, the trustees, Baker and Thomson, renewed the negotiations with Sheffield

15 Meersbrook, home of the Guild's Collection from 1890 until 1953.

16 *Meersbrook: the Picture Gallery, with Bunney's St Mark's on the end wall.*

17 *Meersbrook: The Mineral Room, where casts were also exhibited.*

18 *Meersbrook: The Library. Quotations from Ruskin decorate the frieze. Laying horizontal on rollers in the lower part of the bookcase are the volumes of the Eyton Collection.*

for the re-housing of the Collection. Finally an agreement was signed by which the Guild loaned the Collection to the city on a renewable twenty year lease. It was intended to retain the Walkley premises as a branch or store, but with Swan's death, it was decided to dispose of the house. William White, a professional curator, was appointed to succeed Swan. He took up his duties in February 1890 and within a month everything had been moved to Meersbrook.

At Meersbrook there was plenty of space to exhibit the Collection. But by devoting different rooms to each type of exhibit, White negated many of Ruskin's finer association of exhibits and his comments on various pieces ceased to have meaning.

The new museum was formally opened on Tuesday 15 April 1890 by George Howard, Earl of Carlisle, patron of the arts and a keen amateur artist.

Among those present at the formal ceremony were Alderman and Mrs Baker, Councillor and Mrs Thomson, E. R. Robson, the architect, Albert Fleming, Ruskin's publisher George Allen, his solicitor, H. P. Mackrell, and Joan and Arthur Severn. In his speech Arthur Severn gave Ruskin's apologies for his absence. Severn recounted how he and his wife had been with Ruskin in 1876 when Ruskin had first visited the museum at Walkley and had deplored the lack of space. The new museum proved very popular with the people of Sheffield and in 1891-92 it was visited by more than 61,000 people.

In 1893 William White followed Ruskin's footsteps through Italy and a couple of years later this resulted in the publication of his 634 paged *The Principles of Art as illustrated by Examples in the Ruskin Museum at Sheffield; with passages, by permission, from the writings of John Ruskin.* In it he linked Ruskin's words and his own observations to many of the pictures in the Guild's Collection. This is a valuable work, printed in Sheffield and published by George Allen, which does much to bring the Collection to life.

In 1899 William White disagreed with two members of his Museum's Committee who subsequently "set up utterly false charges against me" and he was dismissed. He was replaced as curator by Gill Parker who continued to care for the Collection for the next thirty two years.

Before the century was over Ruskin's educational theories were being put into practice, notably at the Ruskin School Home at Heacham in Norfolk by Harry Lowerison. In the next century J. Howard Whitehouse was to found Bembridge School in the Isle of Wight and to incorporate into its syllabus all that Ruskin had hoped would be taught at St George's Schools.

19 The page from the National Address of Congratulation to John Ruskin on his eightieth birthday which lists Companions and Artists working for the Guild.

Whitehouse and William Wardle were to meet Ruskin on 8 February 1899 when they took to Brantwood the National Address of Congratulation on his eightieth birthday. They were both to become Companions, with Whitehouse as a Trustee and Wardle as Secretary.

John Ruskin, the founder and first Master of The Guild of St George, died at Coniston on 20 January 1900. At his funeral on 25 January his coffin was draped with a pall made by Marian Twelves and the members of the Ruskin Linen Industry. Four of the six Pall Bearers – George Baker, George Thomson, W. G. Collingwood and George Allen – were Companions of the Guild. Another Companion, Rev. H. D. Rawnsley, wrote a hymn for the service.

2 *The Twentieth century and after*

Following Ruskin's decline into inactivity after 1889 the Guild had become largely dormant. George Baker, a trustee with George Thomson, had assumed the role of Acting Master, but during Ruskin's continuing Mastership, he seems to have taken little action.

It is evident from the Eightieth Birthday Address to Ruskin that there were, in 1899, thirty-three Companions. Many of them were, of course, engaged in their own work. George Allen had been established by Ruskin as his publisher in 1871 when Ruskin set about changing the way in which his, and other people's, books were published. The experiment led to the Net Book Agreement which controlled the way new books were sold for over a century. Allen eventually took on other authors; the firm grew, and developed into the internationally-known firm of George Allen & Unwin Ltd. Their wrought iron sign "Ruskin House" can still be seen hanging over 40 Museum Street in London. The Rev. J .P. Faunthorpe was running Whitelands College, the girls' college in Chelsea where Ruskin had been responsible for establishing a May Queen Festival in 1881, while John Morgan, a dedicated Ruskin writer and collector, was busy with his affairs including running Aberdeen University Press. Canon H. D. Rawnsley was always busy. Influenced by Ruskin as an undergraduate at Oxford, he had become one of the founders of the National Trust. He was vicar of Crosthwaite, Keswick and much involved in all Lakeland activities. He was also engaged in running his Keswick School of Industrial Arts. Egbert Rydings was working with his woollen mill at Laxey and was active in Isle of Man affairs.

In Liverpool a group of Companions, whose activities centred on Mulberry Cottage, and who were practically active in pursuing Ruskin's ideals, feared for the very continued existence of the Guild. John E.Fowler, Clucas Quayle, Emmeline Stapledon, Edith Hope Scott and Violet Wardle wrote to Companions in 1901 drawing their attention to the fact that few other than the Liverpool Companions had attended a previous Guild meeting at Sheffield, and urging them to attend a meeting in Liverpool. As a result, a representative group of Companions met; George Baker was elected Master and William Wardle became the Secretary.

Some of these early Liverpool Companions were to have long family connections with the Guild. The Quayle family connection continues to the present time. C.C.Quayle became a Companion about 1886. His son elder Cuthbert was later enrolled. His younger son, Kendrick, had many business and other commitments and was not enrolled until 1986, just a hundred years after his father! Meanwhile Kendrick's son, Cedric, had already been a Companion since 1969. Three generations of Quayles have cared for our land at

20 Frank Dickinson (1874-1961) was a Companion who built his own house at Carshalton, and made his own furniture. He carved and painted this portrait of Ruskin, and set below it a carved quotation about the Guild onto his panelled wall.

Bewdley. Cedric became a director of the Guild in 1976, resigning in 1992 to become the Company Secretary. He held this office until 2007 when he retired and was immediately re-elected a director.

Such is the dedicated family connection one finds in the Guild. The Wardles are another. William Wardle became a Companion in 1900 and served as Secretary from 1908 until 1925. His son Bernard became a Companion in 1930, was Secretary from 1950 to 1975 and was Acting Master in 1954. William Wardle's grandson, Peter, was enrolled in 1959. Jointly with Cedric Quayle, in 1989, he wrote *Ruskin and Bewdley*, recording much early Guild and family history.

21 St George's Farm, Bewdley from a recent photograph.

In the summer of 1889 Thomas and Margaret Harley had left Liverpool and moved to Bewdley where they had bought a plot of land in the Wyre Forest from George Baker. Here, they reclaimed the land to form a small fruit farm. Later they were followed to Bewdley by other Liverpool Companions, eager to develop the land and forge new lives for themselves.

In 1907 the Guild built a house, to be called St George's Farm, on land already given by Baker. The farm was first let to a local tenant but by 1912 Frederick Watson and his wife, members of the Liverpool Ruskin Society, had moved to Bewdley and became the Guild's tenants. They remained at St George's Farm until 1938 when they returned to Liverpool due to ill health. The tenancy of the farm then passed to Mrs Watson's nephew, Ruskin Williams. He farmed there until 1956 when the tenancy passed to the present tenant, Jack Bishop.

The Guild's Collection was on loan to Sheffield on a renewable lease. In 1910 Baker renewed the lease for a further twenty years. Later in the same year he died at the age of eighty five and his co-trustee, George Thomson, was elected Master in his stead.

George Thomson lived at Huddersfield. His family firm, William Thomson & Sons Ltd, were woollen and worsted millers. The mill employed some 150 people and Thomson re-organised it on what may be called Ruskinian principles. It was a firm in which effectively all of the employees were partners. In 1911, the year after he became Master, George Thomson also became the much respected mayor of Huddersfield. He also seems to have been mayor in the following year.

22 George Thomson, Mayor of Huddersfield and Master, 1910-1920.

In view of Thomson's connection with the woollen industry, it is not surprising that he took an interest in the Guild's textile activities. Almost from the beginning of the Guild's association with Egbert Rydings's mill at Laxey, Thomson was deputed to keep a watching brief on its work. He also took an interest in the Keswick Linen Industry.

To give herself more flexibility Marian Twelves had parted from the Langdale Linen Industry and Albert Fleming, whose housekeeper she was, and had moved to Crosthwaite, near Keswick. Canon Rawnsley was vicar of Crosthwaite. Miss Twelves had been visited there by a number of Companions attending the Guild's meeting in 1902 in the Crosthwaite Parish Room. The Linen Industry by this time was affiliated to the Guild. In 1907 Miss

Twelves took on Miss Ada Hooper as a partner in the business but Miss Twelves was becoming less enamoured with her connection with Rawnsley's many activities. In 1913 the Guild bought a pair of semi-detached cottages in Keswick and she moved from Crosthwaite into these new premises. Over the door was the sign "The Ruskin Linen Industry", and to the right was another sign, "St George's Cottage (Guild of St George)". Four years later Miss Twelves retired and Ada Hooper took charge of the business. Marian Twelves died in 1929 aged 86.

George Thomson retired from the Mastership in 1920 and H.E.Luxmoore was elected to replace him. Henry Elford Luxmoore was an assistant master at Eton. He first met Ruskin on 10 May 1873 when Ruskin lectured at Eton, one of his *Love's Meinie* lectures on Greek

23 Miss Marian Twelves, spinning, outside the Ruskin Linen Industry cottage at Keswick.

24 A group of Companions photographed after an AGM at Meersbrook. H.E.Luxmoore, Master 1920-1925 (wearing hat). J.Howard Whitehouse (with folded arms), a Trustee until 1955.

25

and English birds, and again a week later when he returned to lecture on "The Chough". A correspondence ensued, and in 1883 Luxmoore became a Companion. Luxmoore was much involved with his long and close connection with the college and his public interests in Eton and Windsor. In view of this, and of his age, he reluctantly agreed to be Master for a year, but this stretched to five years and he retired in 1925.

In his annual report for 1924 he noted that the Guild's picture gallery was "somewhat crowded" and he hoped for more space. Also at Sheffield, St George's Farm at Totley was producing vegetables and fruit, mainly for local requirements as Ruskin had wished. St George's Cottages at Barmouth were "very small and the rents are very low". He also reported that the Guild had given a "Ruskin Library" to the High School at Barmouth and each year they gave a Ruskin Drawing Prize. Ruskin books were also given to Kidderminster High School, and of course to Whitelands College. Allen & Unwin had re-issued *Readings from Fors Clavigera*

25 *The group of cottages at Barmouth, North Wales, which Mrs Talbot gave to the Guild in 1875.*

and presentation copies had been sent to "all Training Colleges and many of the principal schools. The book has been welcomed in Japan."

On H. E. Luxmoore's retirement from the Mastership in 1925, Hugh C. Fairfax-Cholmeley was elected to replace him. Fairfax-Cholmeley, of Hoveringham, York, was an old friend of Luxmoore and the father of two of Luxmoore's Eton pupils. Fairfax-Cholmeley brought to the work of the Guild a wide knowledge of country life and a deep interest in the revival of craftsmanship, and in the promotion of agricultural co-operation.

Indeed this period of Mastership did see a number of developments and changes. One important change was the retirement of the Secretary, William Wardle. He had held the office since 1902, and when he retired in 1925 Harrison Ruskin Fowler succeeded him and the Guild arranged to share a single office with the Institute of Sociology, based at that time at Le Play House in Westminster. The Institute was formed by Alexander Farquharson. In it were merged several other organisations, including *The Sociological Review* and the work of such people as Patrick Geddes, Victor Brandford and the French sociologist Le Play. Farquharson was the director of the Institute and he became much involved in the running of the Guild, with the Institute eventually taking on the Secretaryship.

Consideration was given to the Guild's land holdings and a number of changes were made. St George's Farm at Totley was sold to its tenant. At Bewdley, Uncllys Farm and some adjacent land was bought from Peter Adam who by now

26 Uncllys Farm, Bewdley, photographed in 2010.

owned Beaucastle. Consideration was given to the desirability of retaining the Barmouth cottages; in the event they were not disposed of. With the death of Marian Twelves in 1929 the Guild became responsible for the control of the Linen Industry.

There were developments too with the Collection. When Ruskin bought Verrocchio's *Madonna and Child* painting for the Guild, it was in need of restoration and he had it transferred from its original wooden panel to canvas. Now it needed further restoration and this was carried out. Finally, in 1931 Gill Parker, who had been the Collection's Curator since 1899, retired due to ill health, and his assistant, Miss Genevieve Pilley became Acting Curator.

It was during this period that Mrs Mary Greg was enrolled as a Companion. She was connected to the family which owned Quarry Bank Mill at Styal in Cheshire (now owned by the National Trust). Mrs Greg was to become a very generous donor to the Guild.

When he retired in 1934 Hugh Fairfax-Cholmeley's elected successor was T. Edmund Harvey. Harvey had long been influenced by Ruskin's ideals and had been a Companion since about 1902. He was a member of the London County Council from 1904 to 1907 and Warden of Toynbee Hall in east London from 1906 to 1911. In 1910 he entered parliament as the Liberal member for Leeds and between 1914 and 1920 he was engaged in relief work in the war zone in France on behalf of the Society of Friends. In 1923-4 he was the M.P. for Dewsbury and from 1937 to 1945 he was the member representing the Combined Universities.

27 T.Edmund Harvey, Master 1934-1951, probably photographed in his early days as an M.P.

The Guild was to see many changes and developments during Harvey's Mastership. Two long-standing Companions died in 1936-7. Edith Hope Scott was one of the Liverpool group of Companions. She had been enrolled in the 1880s and had visited Ruskin at Brantwood in 1883 and again in 1898. In 1908 she moved to a house in the Wyre Forest which her father had built for her. She was the author of some dozen books, the most significant being her *Ruskin's Guild of St George*, published by Methuen's in 1931.

Juliet Morse, whose death was recorded in the 1936-7 Annual Report, was one of the earliest Companions. Ruskin had listed her name on his 1876 Roll. When she was a child Ruskin had taught her to paint. She was the daughter of geologist Alfred Tylor of Carshalton. Tyler had helped Ruskin in 1872 when he arranged for the cleaning and beautifying of a polluted spring in the village, one of the sources of the river Wandle, and dedicated it to his mother's memory, as "Margaret's Well" in the village. Ruskin described

Juliet as "a rich girl but a very nice one". She may have known Rose La Touche because she gave Ruskin's miniature portrait of Rose to the Guild's Collection.

In 1938-9 electricity was installed in the Barmouth cottages and there being no prospect of the Linen Industry being revived, the decision was taken to sell the Keswick cottages. They were bought at valuation by J. Howard Whitehouse, one of the Guild's trustees.

28 John Ruskin's miniature watercolour portrait of Rose La Touche, c.1872, given to the Guild by Mrs Sydney Morse.

The war brought its own problems for the Collection. "The chief treasures" of the Collection were moved to a place of greater safety, but much of the Collection remained at Meersbrook and the 1939-40 Annual Report assured Companions that the museum still contained "very many beautiful pictures, casts of sculpture, minerals and valuable books". In fact the Collection had just been enriched by the gift of in excess of 120 engravings and mezzotints by Turner and Frank Short. These had been assembled by Stopford W. W. Brooke, son of the well-known divine.

In September 1949 Mrs Greg died aged almost 100. She was one of the Guild's most generous benefactors. Among her gifts was a small 16th century painting of an angel's head, the two volumes of her own Nature Diary, a beautifully written quotation from *Deucalion*, a fine mahogany bookcase, a bungalow in Devon, and nine houses at Westmill, near Buntingford in Hertfordshire.

Our Collection, of course, was leased to Sheffield on a renewable lease. This lease expired in 1950 and although Sheffield wished to keep the Collection in the city, it was

29 The village green at Westmill, with some of the Guild's houses.

announced that Meersbrook would no longer be available because the city could not afford to undertake the necessary restoration of the building. At first it was hoped to build an addition to the Mappin Gallery to house the Collection, but building regulations proved to be a stumbling block. The city regretted that it may not be possible to meet the Guild's desire to keep all of the Collection in one place and at the end of March 1953 Meersbrook was closed. The Collection was put into storage, but it was hoped to be able to exhibit selected items from time to time at the Graves Gallery, or elsewhere.

During this period of uncertainty as to the future of the Collection, T. Edmund Harvey felt he had to resign the Mastership after seventeen years in office. Alexander Farquharson, who had effectively been the Secretary since the Guild's administration was combined with that of the Institute of Sociology, was elected to replace him.

The arrangement for keeping the Collection in Sheffield was an unsatisfactory one and the Master set about looking for a new home. Preliminary discussions were held with Edinburgh and Reading universities. J. Howard Whitehouse offered space at Brantwood which he had established as a Ruskin memorial. Finally it was decided that Reading would be the most suitable home for the Collection. It was considered that its association with a university

30 Bernard Wardle, Acting Master 1954, and Secretary for a number of years.

atmosphere would provide stability and Reading was considered to be the ideal because it had a strong School of Art and "several professors at Reading have strong Ruskin interests". The university's Museum of Rural Life was also a draw.

During Farquharson's Mastership the Institute of Sociology experienced serious financial problems. Finally in 1954 the affairs of the Institute were wound up, its assets transferred to the Guild and Bernard Wardle, the son of William Wardle, became the Secretary.

Farquharson improved the financial status of the Guild by revising its Memorandum and Articles of Association thus enabling it to be recognised as a charity for purposes of income tax.

Alexander Farquharson was suffering from ill-health and in December 1953 he announced a meeting in the following spring at which he would retire and a new Master would be elected. In the event he died before this meeting could be held and the Secretary, Bernard Wardle assumed the role of Acting Master.

Bernard Wardle's months as Acting Master were fraught with the difficulties of the move of the Collection, the closing down of the Institute of Sociology, and the changes in our financial status. His work did not cease in September 1954 when Professor H.A.Hodges of Reading University was elected as the new Master because at the same meeting Bernard Wardle resumed the role of Secretary.

31 St George's Field at Sheepscombe in Gloucestershire preserved as a haven for wild flowers and butterflies which was given to the Guild in 1937 by Miss Margaret Knight. © Robert Wolstenholme.

It was during this period that T. Edmund Harvey died in May 1955 and Mrs Harvey died later in the same year. Lord Courtauld Thomson, one of the Trustees, died towards the end of 1954 and J. Howard Whitehouse, the other Trustee, died in September 1955, having been a Companion since 1902.

Further difficulties arose in relation to the Guild's status and throughout 1960 negotiations continued between the Guild, the Charity Commissioners and the Board of Trade. These eventually led to another revision of our Memorandum and Articles of Association. In these the Guild's objects were re-defined as being:

> To promote the advancement of education and training in the fields of rural economy, industrial design and craftsmanship, and appreciation of the arts, in accordance with

the principles set out in the *Letters to Working Men* by John Ruskin published under the title of *Fors Clavigera*.

Not until an Extraordinary General Meeting in October 1970 were the revised Memorandum and Articles adopted, and the Guild was again recognised as a charity. The revision of the Articles meant that the responsibilities of the Master were in future to be shared by a Board of Directors of which the Master was chairman. The first directors were Bernard Wardle, Mark Harvey (nephew of T. Edmund Harvey), Professor Betts and Jon Thompson, with Cedric Quayle, Professor Holt and Peter Fitzgerald soon also being elected.

In 1949 Genevieve Pilley, who had been acting curator of our Collection since 1931 retired and Dr Richard Seddon who was in overall charge of Sheffield's museums and galleries began to take a personal interest. By 1954 he had completed an up to date inventory of the Collection and an agreement was signed with the city that the

32 Edward Lear's watercolour of a Comb Duck, c.1837, one of the very many images of birds in the Guild's Eyton Collection.

Collection should remain in storage in Sheffield indefinitely. The city was allowed to exhibit items occasionally, and during the period 1950 to 1963 many loans were made to exhibitions in London and elsewhere.

But this was a situation that could not continue and finally the decision was taken to move the collection from Sheffield to Reading. The greater part moved in 1963; one or two items were temporarily left in Sheffield, including the "Ruskin Madonna" by Verrocchio. Later in the same year the library was moved, and early in 1964 the rest of the Collection moved to its new home. Four years later Catherine Williams was appointed Research Fellow and her work ultimately led to the publication in 1984 of *John Ruskin:*

Late Work 1870-1890. The Museum and Guild of St George: An Educational Experiment, a valuable volume containing much early history and a catalogue of the pictures in the Collection.

During this period there were also changes to the Guild's real estate. In 1963 the bungalow at Holcombe in Devon which formed part of the Greg Bequest was sold to the tenant's daughter. In 1971 there was trouble with the Barmouth property which was built onto the hillside. A retaining wall collapsed, destroying one or two outbuildings and damaging an adjacent property. Repairs were completed in the following year and the decision was taken to sell all of the Barmouth property to the local council.

In the following year the Verrocchio painting was moved to London for restoration by John Brealey. After the revision of the Memorandum the Guild had considered the possibility of selling the painting in order to raise sufficient capital to implement its future work. Eventually it was decided to sell the painting and in 1975 it was bought by the National Gallery of Scotland in Edinburgh, with the help of the National Art Collections Fund. In the following year Bernard Wardle gave up the Secretaryship and was succeeded by the Bursar of Reading University, R. H. Giddings.

At Reading the housing of the Collection was unsatisfactory. Responsibility was divided between the Fine Art Department and the Library. The books and much of the furniture were in a room in the Library, and most of the remainder was stored in cellars in a wing of the old Library building. Eventually a committee under the chairmanship of Professor Cyril Tyler, the Vice-Chancellor, was set up to seek a way of housing everything together and in 1972 the whole Collection was reunited in a wing of the old Library building. Mrs Andrea Finn was appointed Curator under the supervision of Peter Fitzgerald of the Fine Art Department.

33 Professor Cyril Tyler, Master 1973-1977.

The Guild's association with Reading had not been entirely satisfactory. In December 1977 the Master, Professor Tyler, and the Secretary resigned.

Once again Bernard Wardle acted as Secretary, and Jon Thompson, Dean of the School of Art and Design at London University's Goldsmiths' College, was elected Master. By a happy chance J. P. Cordery who had been the Guild's auditor for a number of years retired from his accountancy firm and took on the role of Secretary, which he carried out successfully until October 1992 when Cedric Quayle resigned his directorship to take over as Secretary.

Jon Thompson's Mastership was marked by a number of innovations made possible by the new much increased income resulting from well-invested funds from the sale of the Verrocchio.

34 Corn Ball, c.8" diameter, by Andy Goldsworthy. There are other examples of Goldsworthy's work in the Collection together with examples of craftsmanship by others who received Guild awards.

35 The first design of an insignia by Edward Burne-Jones for the title pages of Ruskin's Bibliotheca Pastorum series of books intended for the libraries on Guild lands. By the time Ruskin was satisfied with the designs, the books had been printed using another insignia. A re-drawing of this first design is now used on the covers of the Guild's annual Ruskin Lectures.

An annual Ruskin Lecture was introduced in 1978, with Asa Briggs, now one of our senior Companions, delivering the first in the series. Some lectures were delivered in London, some in Sheffield, or elsewhere. The intention was also to print the lecture, and while this has not always been possible, a valuable series has been produced.

A series of annual Craft Awards was instituted in association with the Crafts Council. Academic Awards were also introduced, and we were occasionally able to make small grants to suitable applicants. In 1979 we helped the Bewdley Museum establish its brass foundry.

In the early days of the Guild, Companions had kept in touch with each other's activities through *Fors Budget*. This was a hand-written journal passed from Companion to Companion with each recipient adding a paragraph or two before sending it on its way. It was begun in 1895 and helped to keep the Guild together during Ruskin's declining years. This journal eventually lapsed and in 1977 a new *Guild of St George Newsletter*, edited by Mark Harvey, first appeared. Mark edited it for ten years; he was followed as editor by Betty Nicolson, and then by Rita Lenney. Anthony Harris issued three short *Newsletters* in 1992 when the series ended. Between November 1993 and November 1994 Philip Barnes edited several issues of '*Fors*'. *The Letters of the Companions of the Guild of St George*. Then there was a gap before the Guild's current annual journal, *The Companion*, first appeared in 2001. I have to admit responsibility for the title and the first editor was John Spiers; after three years Francis O'Gorman took over, and three years later Graham Parry became the editor.

By the beginning of 1979 Reading was showing little interest in making the Collection available to the general public, and Sheffield was showing signs of wishing to have it returned to the city. A year later the Guild told the Reading authorities that it was intended to withdraw the Collection in two years time. Their response was that if it was withdrawn immediately it would release valuable space to the university.

Accordingly in July 1981 a new agreement was signed with Sheffield City Council for the return of the Guild's Collection to the city. The original intention was that Sheffield would build an extension to the Mappin Gallery in Weston Park to house the Collection, but this of course would take time. Meanwhile the Collection returned to Sheffield where it was put into storage.

Jon Thompson retired as Master in 1982 and in his place Anthony Harris was elected. By chance the Reading association was continued in that the new Master had studied art and cost accountancy at Reading and became interested in Ruskin through seeing the Collection there. He became a Companion in 1973 and a director of the Guild in 1977. He had studied at the Courtauld and had been at St Albans School of Art before becoming Vice Principal of Chelsea School of Art in 1976, from where, between 1986 and 1989 he went to Camberwell School of Art as Principal.

The new agreement with Sheffield included their need to appoint a Keeper for the Collection and David Alston, then Assistant Keeper of the Christ Church Art Collection at Oxford, was appointed.

Frank Constantine, who was a Guild director and Director of Arts in Sheffield had been a prime mover in the return of the Collection. He was about to retire from his City appointment and his deputy, Julian Spalding, also a Guild director, was appointed to replace him. David Alston was promoted to become Deputy Director, and Janet Barnes, who had been working with the Collection while it was in storage, was appointed the new Keeper. This was an appointment which she was to occupy with great success until 1995 when she left Sheffield to become the Director of the Crafts Council.

Meanwhile plans for a new gallery had run into difficulty. Since the Mappin Gallery was a listed building, planning permission to build an additional gallery there had not been forthcoming. By happy chance the council owned the old Hayes Wine Store in Norfolk Street in the centre of the city. This was empty and the decision was taken to turn this into the very attractive new Ruskin Gallery. An iron staircase and mezzanine floor balustrade, and window bars, were commissioned from Giuseppe Lund who was later to make the Queen Elizabeth

36 The Ruskin Gallery in Norfolk Street, 1985-2001. Giuseppe Lund's staircase and ballustrade can be seen.

Gates in London. David Kindersley was commissioned to design and cut a large name tablet to go at the entrance to the gallery and Lida Lopes Cardozo, his wife and partner, produced very attractive exhibit labels. The new Ruskin Gallery was formally opened by Lord Strabolgi, Opposition Spokesman for the Arts, in 1985. In the following year the Gallery

37 Anthony Harris, Master 1982-1996, with Janet Barnes (Keeper, left) and Jeanne Clegg, an exhibition curator, at the opening of the Ruskin and Tuscany exhibition in Lucca.

was entered for the Museum of the Year Award and received the Sotheby Award for the Best Museum of Fine and Applied Arts.

Jon Thomson's innovations were continued. Agricultural grants and awards were begun under the aegis of Andrew Jewell, director and retired director of Reading's Museum of Rural Life. Other directors at this time were Henry King whose expertise in the care of old buildings made him an ideal director for properties. Cedric Quayle, whose family had long Guild connections, looked after the Bewdley properties; Mark Harvey, nephew of the former Master, always gave wise advice. The present writer provided the connection with the academic Ruskin world

38 The last Directors' Meeting in the Norfolk Street Library on 16 June 2000. Left to right: Mark Harvey, Cedric Quayle (Secretary), Julian Spalding, Master 1996-2005, Anthony Page.

and was instrumental in renewing the Guild's connection with the May Queen ceremony and tradition at Whitelands College at Putney. To emphasise the Guild's interest in crafts, part of the Norfolk Street building was opened as a Craft Gallery in 1988.

In 1993 the Guild sponsored a major Ruskin exhibition. This was curated by Paul Tucker, a Pisan Ruskin scholar, and Dr Jeanne Clegg who had been based in Rome for some time. *Ruskin and Tuscany*, with scholarly catalogues in English and Italian editions, opened at the Accademia Italiana delle Arti in London in January-February; between February and April the exhibition was in Sheffield and then it travelled to Italy where it was shown in May and June at the Fondazione Ragghianti in Lucca.

Following the success of the *Ruskin and Tuscany* exhibition, for several years the Guild offered two bursaries to artists aged over forty for travel to and living expenses at the Fattoria Colle Verde near Lucca. Subsequently their work was shown in Sheffield at the Graves Art Gallery.

Camilla Hampshire replaced Janet Barnes as our Keeper in 1995 and in the following year Anthony Harris retired as Master. Julian Spalding was elected to replace him. He had gone from Sheffield to be Director of Manchester Art Gallery, and from there to be responsible for the group of museums and galleries in Glasgow. His former connection with Sheffield and his intimate knowledge of the workings of the museums world were great assets.

The work of the Guild continued, but our original post-Verrocchio investments had now largely fallen due and the re-invested capital did not produce the income of the palmier days of the 1970s and '80s. We had already sold one of our houses in Westmill. The tenant of another small cottage had died and the building was dramatically in need of restoration. Anthony Page, now our director for properties, had plans drawn for a new suitable house and we sold the old cottage for demolition and with planning permission.

Julian Spalding brought an excellent new idea to the Guild, a Campaign for Drawing. Like Ruskin, we had always considered drawing as vital to "seeing" and we discovered a decline in the teaching of drawing in schools. The aim of the Campaign was to persuade more people to draw. Sue Grayson Ford, recently retired director of London's Serpentine Gallery, ran the Campaign for us. It was spectacularly successful and within a few years thousands of

39 A view of the Ruskin Gallery in Sheffield's Millennium Gallery complex, before it was re-designed in 2010.

people were participating in drawing events being held worldwide. The Guild supported the Campaign for a number of years, while it also attracted much other financial support.

Part of Sheffield's plans to celebrate the millennium was the erection of a new gallery complex in the city centre. The new Millennium Galleries, a range of four galleries connected by a precinct leading from Arundel Gate to the new Winter Garden, was opened in 2001. As part of this scheme the city intended selling our Norfolk Street gallery, and making one of the new galleries available for the Collection.

The new gallery is smaller than the former premises and we have always had more material in the Collection than we could exhibit. This situation was now worse, and in order to be able to show parts of the Collection unseen for some years, the Master devised a scheme for a series of three major exhibitions held at three yearly intervals, to be known as the Ruskin Triennial Exhibitions. Our sponsorship of the series was due to begin with the ending of our Campaign sponsorship.

By now Dorian Church had succeeded Camilla Hampshire in 2001 as our Keeper, and in March 2004 Louise Pullen, now our Curator, was engaged to produce a completely new catalogue of the Collection. In January 2009 our present Keeper, Kim Streets, was appointed.

Julian Spalding resigned from the Mastership in 2005 and in that year the present writer succeeded him, saying that he in turn would retire when the first of the Triennial Exhibitions was opened.

Coinciding with my election was the disturbing news of the dramatic decline in the numbers of wild flowers in the country. I felt that this was something that would have disturbed Ruskin, and we determined to try to do something about it. We found that the National Trust was already managing certain

40 *A field of Betony at Uncllys Farm, Bewdley.*

of its properties in a wild-flower-friendly way. This type of management was not land-cost-effective, and for a couple of years we helped to sponsor experiments on some of their lands, thereafter moving our sponsorship to the Wyre Community Land Trust, a similar scheme operating in the Wyre Forest. This is masterminded by our director John Iles who is also our tenant at Uncllys Farm. His sympathetic care of the land at Uncllys and elsewhere in the forest is fostering the regeneration of wild flowers in the area.

The series of annual Ruskin Lectures had lapsed, and I reintroduced them, beginning in 2005 with a lecture by Stephen Wildman on T. M. Rooke, one of the artists commissioned by Ruskin to work for the Guild. Our annual general meetings for a number of years had been held in Sheffield and some

41 (Left to right) John Iles, Clive Wilmer, the present Master, Robert Wilson, James S. Dearden, Master 2005-2009, Peter Miller, Cedric Quayle, Norman Hobbs (Secretary) in Ruskin's former Rooms at Corpus Christi College, Oxford, on 14 November 2008, following a Directors' Meeting.

Companions wanted a change; accordingly during the next few years we held meetings at Cambridge, Oxford and Bewdley.

The first in the series of Triennial Exhibitions, "Can Art Save Us?" was opened in October 2009. It was a very successful culmination of four years' work and sponsorship, and it was very well received.

At the annual general meeting, also held in Sheffield in the following month, I retired as Master, and the present Master, Clive Wilmer of Sidney Sussex College, Cambridge, was elected as my successor.

As I write, developments are taking place at Bewdley. An unattractive barn at Uncllys Farm has been pulled down and John Iles has replaced it with a fine new Ruskin Studio, built in traditional style using oak from the Guild's land. It has been equipped with Guild furniture originally made for the Walkley museum. Here many visitors will come to learn about and enjoy all that goes on in the forest, and be refreshed by "the pure air of Bewdley".

The orchard at St George's Farm is old and rather derelict. Cedric Quayle has a plan of the orchard drawn in 1880 which shows and names each individual tree. Perhaps one day this will enable us to re-plant at least some of it as it used to be.

The Guild also looks forward to the future when we may be able to collaborate with the Bewdley Museum, to exhibit part of our Collection there.

Ruskin's original concept for the Guild was that it should consist

> ... of a body of people who think ... that the sum which well-disposed persons usually set aside for charitable purposes (namely, a tenth part of their income) may be most usefully applied in buying land for the nation, and entrusting the cultivation of it to a body of well-taught and well cared-for peasantry. For the teaching of these labourers, schools are to be erected, with museums and libraries in fitting places ...

Ruskin's was an ambitious plan, which he adapted to suit the circumstances (the annual tithe was soon dropped, Companions contributing what they could), and his ideals and ideas are still being adapted to suit modern needs. But here at Bewdley the Guild is able to come nearest to putting Ruskin's original concept into practice.

42 The Ruskin Studio at Uncllys Farm, just before its opening in 2010.

3 The Collection of The Guild of St George

Writing of the Guild's Collection in the *Manchester Guardian* of 20 April 1956 Norman Shrapnell said:

> John Ruskin deposited a queer magpie-hoard in darkest Sheffield – bits of quartz and precious stones, illuminated missals, glittering records in paint of Venetian palaces and details of mosaics ...

The Collection *is* diverse but is representative of Ruskin's many and varied interests. It was his hope that the differing exhibits would give new interests to, and help to educate, the visitors to the Guild's museum. The many and diverse items in the Collection can all variously be related to each other, and it was Ruskin's intention that they should also be *seen* together. They *were* as far as possible, exhibited in this way at Walkley, and are again now in our present gallery. At Meersbrook, where there was more space, the exhibits were categorised and given their own galleries. In order to give some idea of the scope and range of the Collection, I propose to categorise them here.

In general terms, the original Collection comprises pictures, prints, casts, coins, minerals and precious stones, medieval manuscripts and printed books. Since Ruskin's time, the Collection has been broadened by gifts and bequests usually from Companions, and by gifts or purchases from craftsmen and artists sponsored by the Guild. Having established his museum and begun to collect for it, it had to be furnished. The Guild commissioned chairs, tables, display tables and bookcases. Ruskin had a double mahogany cabinet of sliding frames, based on the design of those he commissioned for the

43 Ruskin probably met Raffaelle Carloforti in Assisi in 1874. He was soon commissioned to make this study of the head of the recumbent effigy of S.Simeone in the church of S.Simeone Grande, Venice.

43

Ruskin Drawing School Collection, made to contain watercolours and photographs.

The confused state of Ruskin's accounts and his buying methods make it difficult to be certain how and when many items came into the Collection. Sometimes they were given by Ruskin from his own collection; sometimes he bought them for himself and subsequently gave or sold them to the Guild. Other items were bought directly by the Guild (on the instructions of the Master) and on other occasions they were bought by Ruskin on behalf of the Guild.

44 Carloforti's watercolour of Noah from the Vine Angle of Venice's Ducal Palace was probably intended for the Guild Collection but it was never sent on from Brantwood. It is now in the Ruskin Library at Lancaster University.

Space at Sheffield could not keep up with the rapid growth of the Collection. Some material was stored by George Baker in his house at Bewdley; later, some was stored in the Town Clerk's office in Sheffield. Bunney's large study of the west front of St Mark's, Venice, was loaned to Whitelands College until the Walkley extension was built. Other commissions were stored at Brantwood, and indeed some never went from Brantwood to Sheffield and ultimately were included in the Brantwood dispersal sales of 1930-31. Indeed for some time the Guild did not know that the manuscript volume containing the original Roll of Companions had been in one of the sales and had gone to the British Museum.

Ruskin commissioned a group of young artists to make studies for the Collection. Principally they were J. W. Bunney, Charles Fairfax Murray, T. M. Rooke, Frank Randal, H. R. Newman, H. Stacy Marks and two Italians, Angelo Alessandri and Raphaelle Carloforti. Additionally the architect Giacomo Boni and the sculptor Giuseppe Giordani helped with casts and other work. There are also groups or individual pictures which were given or bought.

45 *J.W.Bunney's watercolour of the Loggia of the Palazzo del Consiglio, Verona, 1869. The cornice in the picture was probably altered by Ruskin.*

46 *H.R.Newman, watercolour of roses made at Florence in the spring of 1881.*

45

47 W.G.Collingwood accompanied Ruskin on an Italian tour in 1882. He made this study of a sculptured pilaster in the porch of the Duomo at Lucca.

48 A watercolour study by Charles Fairfax Murray of a 12th century mosaic in St Mark's, Venice, 1877. Ruskin considered this group of life-sized figures "the most precious historical picture of any in worldly gallery or unworldly cloister". Unfortunately Murray omitted to copy the inscription above the figures, "Pontifices. Clerus. Populus. Dux mente serenus" [the Priests, the Clergy, the People. The Duke, serene of mind]. Ruskin later com-missioned T.M.Rooke to make a second copy (now in the Ruskin Library at Lancaster) to include the words.

49 John Ruskin's study showing the sculptural form of a Spray of dead oak leaves, a study of abstract beauty probably made in 1879 at Albert Fleming's house as a lesson for Susan Beever. It was bequeathed by her to Fleming and given by him to the Guild in 1893.

50 Ruskin's watercolour of a Peacock's breast feather, 1873. "I have to draw a peacock's breast feather and paint as much of it as I can, without having heaven to dip my brush in".

51 *Ruskin sent Frank Randal to Ravenna in 1884 to make studies of some of the famous 6th century mosaics in the church of S.Vitale. These roundels contain the images of SS.Bartholomew and Matthew.*

52 *T.M.Rooke's view of the cathedral at Chartres towering above the river, with its washing sheds on either bank, 1885.*

For example, Ruskin gave twelve of his own drawings and watercolours, studies which are a cross-section of his life's work including a large panorama of the Alps, the eastern corner of the Spina Chapel in Pisa, studies from Carpaccio's *St George and the Dragon*, a spray of dead oak leaves and a peacock's breast feather. Ruskin's portrait miniature of Rose La Touche was given by Mrs Sydney Morse. Later, the Guild bought a group of Ruskin's drawings for *The Seven Lamps of Architecture* and some studies which he made during his work on *The Stones of Venice*; in 1991 the Guild bought Ruskin's dramatic study of the Towers of Thun. Ruskin admired the work of the caricature artist John Leech, and he bought over ninety of his drawings for *Punch* and other publications.

53 *Henry Stacy Marks made a speciality of bird studies. This study of the heads of two Tucans was made at London Zoo on 17 October 1877.*

The pictures which Ruskin commissioned fall largely into distinct classes. There are studies from Old Masters, studies of architecture, architectural details and stained glass, landscapes, minerals, and natural history. Additionally there is a series of studies of mosaics at St Mark's, made by T. M. Rooke in 1879 when the originals were threatened with destruction through restoration. Many of Rooke's studies were destroyed in a fire on the Cenis railway during his return journey but his tracings were saved and he was able to make new drawings for the Guild and for the Oxford collection. Altogether the work of forty five artists is represented in the Collection.

In addition to oils, watercolours and drawings, there is a large number of prints in the Collection. Among the artists represented are Albrecht Dürer (seven small prints including three of St George, and six large engravings) and by Turner's *Liber Studiorum* prints, and engravings for other works.

Ruskin considered sculpture to be "the foundation and school of painting, but painting, if first studied, prevents, or at least disturbs, the understanding of the qualities of sculpture". Additionally Ruskin considered that, often, sculpture could be seen to the best advantage in a well-lit cast.

Very many casts of architectural details were made for Ruskin in the 1850s when he was working on *The Stones of Venice*. Eventually these were probably all given to the Architectural Museum in London and many of them have ended up in the Victoria and Albert Museum. In Venice in 1876 Ruskin commissioned many more casts of sculpture and architectural decoration for the Guild. Giuseppe Giordani

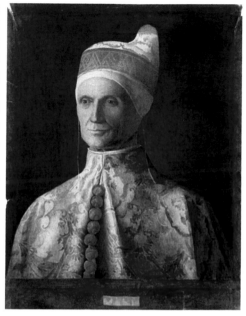

54 Ruskin trained Octavia Hill as a copyist. Her study of Bellini's Portrait of Doge Leonardo Loredan was made in the National Gallery about 1859. Later she helped Ruskin with his housing projects and went on to become one of the founders of the National Trust.

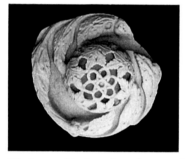

made a cast of Noah's hand unwisely gathering grapes, from the Vine Angle of the Ducal Palace at a cost of £20. There are also casts of capitals (or details) and four large casts of the flying angels on the porch pediments of the Giant's Staircase. These casts of the 14th-15th century work were made before the subsequent 'restoration'.

55 A cast of the boss from the central archivolt on the west front of St Mark's Venice. Ruskin described the original as "the most instructive piece of sculpture of all I ever show".

There are also a number of casts of details of 12th-13th century sculpture on the west front of St Mark's.

At Rouen, Arthur Burgess arranged for the photography of the entire north porch on the west front of the cathedral. The prints are at Sheffield, while the large plate negatives are in the Ruskin Library, Lancaster University. He also made two charcoal studies of carvings, and arranged for casts to be made from many of the 12th-13th century French Gothic sculptures. When the present Ruskin Gallery was first laid out, it incorporated a real-size Rouen arch constructed from Burgess's photographs.

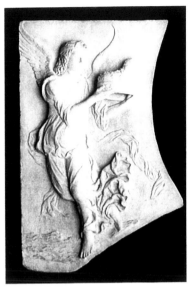

56 *A cast of one of the four flying angels bearing emblems of the State from the pediments of the porches of the Giant's Staircase in the courtyard of Venice's Ducal Palace.*

I referred earlier to William White's 1893 tour of Italy. In the course of this tour he amassed a collection of some 250 of photographs which now form an important study collection and complement the photographs which Ruskin placed in the Collection. The photographs are principally of art and architecture, with an emphasis on Venice.

Displayed at Meersbrook in the Casts Gallery one also found a collection of minerals. Ruskin had been a keen collector of minerals since he was a small boy. He had a fine collection of his own, and he had given collections of minerals to the museums in Coniston and Kirkcudbright, to St David's

57 *A noble opal in the matrix, from Hungary, polished on the edge, "the fiery parts especially are of highest possible jewellers' quality. Ruskin also described this specimen as "at least unexcelled in England".*

58 Ruskin planned but never wrote an historical account of Switzerland
but he did make a number of drawings as part of the scheme. His strik-
ing study of the Walls and Towers of Thun was made in the 1850s.
It was bought by the Guild in 1991.

59 Part of the façade and campanile of
S.Nicola, Pisa, 1882, by Angelo Alessandri.
It has been suggested that this building has
some influence on Southall's design for the
Bewdley Museum.

60 Angelo Alessandri made this study after Tintoretto's Meeting of the Virgin and St Elizabeth with St Zachary in the Sculoa di S.Rocco in Venice in 1880. The copy of the same painting which Burne-Jones made for Ruskin in 1862 is in the Ruskin Library at Lancaster.

61 The façade of the Duomo of S.Martino, Lucca, an 1885 watercolour by H.R.Newman, bought for the Guild two years later.

53

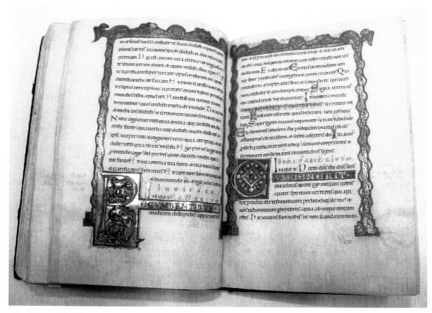

62 One of the finest manuscripts in the Guild's collection: a Lectionary written at the German abbey of Ottobeuren, c.1153-70.

School, Reigate and to Christs Hospital. He gave a substantial number of examples of native silica to the British Museum, and in 1887 he gave them the 130 carat uncut "Colenso Diamond" and the "Edwardes Ruby", both of which were stolen a number of years ago. It is therefore not surprising that a collection of minerals and precious stones was assembled for the Guild. This collection comprises silicious minerals (flint, chalcedony, agates, jasper, etc.), precious metals (gold, silver, platinum), "useful" metals (iron, copper, tin, lead, etc.), precious stones (sapphire, ruby, topaz, emerald, lapis-lazuli, etc.) and others. Many of the exhibits were drawn from his own collection; others were bought for the Guild.

Coins really fall into the same category as sculpture, and Ruskin gave an interesting collection of these to the museum, writing of the

63 J.W.Bunney's study of The West Front of St Mark's,Venice, was commissioned by Ruskin in January 1877 for £500. It was feared that the façade was about to be "restored" and Ruskin wanted a record of its original state. The picture was begun in June 1877 and finally completed in 1882. It was the largest picture painted by Bunney and he worked on it for an estimated 1820 hours, about 1760 being in the Piazza, before finishing the work in his studio.

educational importance he attached to coins in *Aratra Pentelici* (1872). Thirteen Greek coins came from Ruskin's own collection, and he bought electrotypes of obverse and reverse faces of 230 other examples.

English coins range from silver pennies of Harold and William I to gold sovereigns, half sovereigns, and crowns of Elizabeth I. Most of these coins were bought between 1880 and 1886 from the dealer James Verity. Ruskin had intended to make the collection more extensive, but he was never able to do this.

64 Some of the coins in the Guild's Collection.

In the same class as coins are wax models of seals from King Stephen to Queen Victoria, and thirty bronze medallions of cathedrals made by Jacques Weiner.

As a young man John Wharlton Bunney worked in the offices of Smith Elder & Co., Ruskin's publishers. He attended the drawing classes which Ruskin held at the Working Mens' College, became a professional artist and moved to Italy, eventually settling in Venice. The Guild commissioned ten pictures from him. Bunney died prematurely in 1882 and the remaining contents of his studio stayed with the family. The greater part of this collection passed to the Guild in 2002. It comprises twelve oil paintings, sixty six sketch-books and about 950 watercolours and drawings. The important Bunney Diary, recording many details of his life and contacts in Venice, also became the property of the Guild at the same time, but this is not currently available for study.

Then there is the library. It was always Ruskin's intention that the library should be a leading part of the Collection. As established by Ruskin the library provided a selection of standard literature of the time, in good editions, available to the visitor on open access, together with a collection of rarer printed books, illuminated manuscripts and illustrated works on botany, ornithology and zoology – "a working man's Bodleian Library".

Again this was put together partly from Ruskin's own shelves and partly by purchase. Additionally George Allen gave copies of Ruskin's own

65 This manuscript Homilarium remained in the Spanish abbey where it was written in the 10th century until it was bought, through Bernard Quaritch, for the Guild in 1880. It contains more than 200 elaborate initial letters, more than half of them over 6 inches high. One initial is 16 ½ inches high.

works. Later, many British Museum publications were presented by that institution, and there have been many donations and bequests by Companions. There are books about the various classes of exhibits in the Collection – about manuscripts, about engravings, about Venice and Venetian artists; there are volumes containing engravings of our original Leech drawings, and about the artists admired by Ruskin – Turner, Verrocchio, Carpaccio, Giotto, Bewick, Durer, Tintoretto, and many others.

Several Kelmscott Press books were given by William Morris's widow; there are bindings by T. J. Cobden Sanderson. Included in Albert Fleming's bequest are some 350 of the letters which Ruskin wrote to Susan Beever (including some of those which Fleming edited in *Hortus Inclusus*).

Ruskin was a dedicated collector of medieval manuscripts. He was principally interested in the decoration and the lettering, rather than the text, and over the years he brought together a notable collection. Some of these he gave to the Guild; others he bought, or the Guild bought, for its library. We have twelve manuscript in all. The earliest is a late-10th century *Homilarium* written in a Spanish monastery. It remained there until it was bought by Bernard Quaritch, the dealer who sold it to Ruskin in 1880. There is a fine *Lectionary* written in the second half of the 12th century at Ottobeuren Abbey in Germany; a 14th century Parisian Missal was in the chapel of Charles V in 1380. The "De Croy Hours" contains fourteen large miniatures by a close follower of Jean Fouquet and it was used in the late 16th century as an *album amicorum* by Diane de Croy. Ruskin paid £500 for it in 1881 – "an extravagant price but I think Sheffield will be a little proud of having saved it from going to America".

Finally, in a class of their own, are thirty eight large volumes containing over 6000 drawings and prints of birds. The collection was formed by T. C. Eyton, bringing together prints from many of the important ornithological books by Gould, Audubon, Lear and others. Bought from Quaritch for £500, with the thirty eight volumes came the original volumes from which the prints had been extracted (with some prints still *in situ*), in all seventy three volumes. In addition to these are twenty vellum-bound notebooks, Eyton's catalogue of his collection, and a catalogue of his collection of birds' bones and skulls. A few years later, the Guild bought a number of bird books *by* Eyton including his own annotated copy of one of them.

There is far, far more in the Collection of The Guild of St George than can be mentioned here. But perhaps this can serve to give some small indication of the wealth and scope of the Collection brought together by Ruskin and subsequently augmented by Companions of his Guild of St George and other friends.

66 Cissa Venatoria, two birds by John Gould, a hand-coloured lithograph for his book, Birds of Asia.

Masters of the Guild

1871-1900	John Ruskin
1900-1910	George Baker
1910-1920	George Thomson
1920-1925	H.E.Luxmoore
1925-1934	Hugh C.Fairfax-Cholmeley
1934-1951	T.Edmund Harvey
1951-1954	Alexander Farquharson
1954	D.B.Wardle (acting, February-September)
1954-1973	H.A.Hodges
1973-1977	Cyril Tyler
1977-1982	Jon B.Thompson
1982-1996	Anthony Harris
1996-2005	Julian Spalding
2005-2009	James S. Dearden
2009-	Clive Wilmer

Keepers and Curators

1875-1889	Henry Swan
1890-1899	William White
1899-1931	Gill Parker
1931-1949	Genevieve Pilley (acting)
1949-1963	Richard Seddon
1969-1981	Andrea Finn
1982-1983	David Alston
1983-1995	Janet Barnes
1995-2001	Camilla Hampshire
2001-2009	Dorian Church
2004-	Louise Pullen (Curator)
2009-	Kim Streets (Keeper)

Further reading

Armytage, W.H.G.: *Heavens Below. Utopian experiments in England 1560-1960*. Routledge & Kegan Paul, 1961 (pp.289-304, The Guild of St George)

Atkinson, Blanche: *Ruskin's Social Experiment at Barmouth*. James Clarke [1900]

Benjamin, Frederick A.: *The Ruskin Linen Industry of Keswick*. Michael Moon, 1974

Dearden, James S.: *Further Facets of Ruskin*. Published by the author, 2009 (pp.224-242, 'The Library of the Guild of St George')

Dearden, James S.: *John Ruskin, an illustrated life*. Shire Publications, 2008

Dearden, James S.: *John Ruskin's Camberwell*. Brentham Press/Guild of St George, 1990

Eagles, Stuart: *After Ruskin: The Social and Political Legacies of a Victorian Prophet, 1870-1920*. Oxford University Press, forthcoming, 2010/11

Frost, Mark: *The Lost Companion and John Ruskin's Guild Idea*. Anthem Press, forthcoming 2013

Harris, Anthony: *Why have our little girls large shoes? Ruskin and the Guild of St George*. Guild of St George Ruskin Lecture 1985

Haslam, Sara E.: *John Ruskin and the Lakeland Arts Revival, 1880-1920*. Merton, 2004

Hewison, Robert: *Art and Society. Ruskin in Sheffield 1876*. Guild of St George Ruskin Lecture 1979

Hewison, Robert: *Ruskin on Venice*. Yale University Press, 2009

Hilton, Tim: *John Ruskin*. Yale University Press, 2002

King, Sue: *A Weaver's Tale. The Life & Times of the Laxey Woollen Industry 1860-2010*. St George's Woollen Mills Ltd, 2010

Morley, Catherine W.: *John Ruskin: Late Work 1870-1890. The Museum and Guild of St George*. Garland Publishing, 1984

Scott, Edith Hope: *Ruskin's Guild of St George*. Methuen, 1931

Wardle, Peter, and Quayle, Cedric: *Ruskin and Bewdley*. Guild of St George, revised edition, 2007

Yallop, Jacqueline: *Public and Private. Some Views of the Guild of St George Collection*. Sheffield Galleries & Museums Trust and University of Sheffield, 2003

Most of these books are available for reference in the Guild Library.

Websites
To view items in the Collection:
www.museums-sheffield.org.uk/coresite/html/ruskin.asp

To view a reconstruction of the early museum:
www.ruskinatwalkley.org

The Guild's website:
www.guildofstgeorge.org.uk

Acknowledgements
During the writing of this little book Cedric Quayle has been, as always, unfailingly helpful. His knowledge of the Guild and Bewdley is unparallelled and he has answered many questions. He has also made illustrations 5, 14 and 24 available to me. Clive Wilmer and Norman Hobbs have made a number of valuable suggestions. The greater number of illustrations have come from the Guild Collection and Louise Pullen has been very kind in making these available to me. For help with other illustrations I am indebted to Rebecca Patterson of the Ruskin Library, Lancaster University (1, 19, 35, 44), John Iles (21, 26, 40, 41, 42), Mrs Jo Harvey (27), Mrs Cynthia Wardle (30), Robert Wilson (29), Robert Wolstenholme (31), Kirklees Council (22) and the University of Reading (33).

Other Guild publications

Ruskin Lectures

Van Akin Burd: *Ruskin, Lady Mount Temple and the Spiritualists*, 1982

Anthony Harris: *Why do our little girls have large shoes?* 1985

Sir Roy Shaw: *The Relevance of Ruskin*, 1987

Anthony Harris: *Ruskin and Siena*, 1991

Malcolm Cole: *Be like Daisies*, 1992

Royal W. Leith III: *Ruskin and his American followers in Tuscany*, 1994

Sam Smiles: *Ruskin and Cambridge*, 2006

Jacqueline Yallop: *Our Power to Bequeath*, 2007

Paul Tucker: *Charles Fairfax Murray and Duccio's Maesta*, 2008

Robert Hewison: *Of Ruskin's Gardens*, 2009

Some of the illustrated items from The Guild Collection are available as cards from Norman Hobbs, Guild of St George, Clove Cottage, Mitten Road, Bembridge, Isle of Wight. PO35 5UP